How to Speak Skillfully?

By

Chakrapani Srinivasa

How to Speak Skillfully?

By Chakrapani Srinivasa

About the Author

Chakrapani Srinivasa (Padmaja), Freelance journalist from India possesses Bachelor degree in Engineering (B.E) and Post graduate in Business Management (MBA) with Distinction. He has worked as Associate Editor of 'Naradar' fortnightly journal in Chennai, India. He is the Senior Editor of the journal "The Divineness".

Contributed articles, short stories and travelogues in leading journals like Ananda Vikatan, Kumudam, Savi, Kalki, Dinamani Kadhir, Dinamani daily, Idhayam Pesukirathu, Naradar etc

He has written articles and e books through Smashwords Inc, Kindle Direct Publishing, Atlanta publications, Cooperjal publications (UK), lulu.com, ezinearticles.com, shvoong.com, iproclaim.com (USA) and TCC news (Germany).

He is the Consulting Editor: Contemporary Who's Who-Research Board of Advisers of ABI, USA.

View his books

Click to see my e books published by Amazon
http://www.amazon.com/s/ref=la_B01G3JTQ92_B01G3JT Q92_sr?rh=i%3Abooks&field-author=Chakrapani+Srinivasa&sort=relevance&ie=UTF8

Preface

Speaking with office colleagues, boss and clients in an effective manner is essential for any administrator or manager. Your ideas and vision have to be communicated in the right spirit to achieve your goal. So, communication skill is vital for one and all.

To pass information from one end to the other end and establishing an understanding between them can be termed as 'Communication'.

This is a very important aspect of an organization. Without proper communication, the existence of that organization will be ruined.

The feedback from the receiving end to the sender end should be genuine and effective and in the desired manner.

A communication is a weapon, which has to be handled deftly by any manager and also by the organization.

Without proper utilization of the communication, there is bound to be a calamity in the organization with an irreparable loss.

Dedicated To My Dear Parents

Contents

Tips for Communication Skill

Communication

To pass information from one end to the other end and establishing an understanding between them can be termed as 'Communication'.

This is a very important aspect of an organization. Without proper communication, the existence of that organization will be ruined.

The feedback from the receiving end to the sender end should be genuine and effective and in the desired manner.

An immaculate transmission of meaning can be said to be as 'Communication'.

Communication holds a key role in a Manager's Profession.

His duties such as planning, organizing, monitoring etc are all interviewed with good communication.

To reach the goal desired by the management, an accurate communication technique will be essential.

Or else all the effects will be null and void.

A leader has to deal prudently with this communication weapon for the welfare of the organization.

Key elements of Communication

-Source

-Encoding the message

-Channel

-Interpretation

-Re-transmission

-Disturbance, audibility

The source may be a group of persons or a single individual or a machine. This conveys the desired message to the destination where it should reach.

This information is to be encoded to the other by means of language or actions. The verbal and non-verbal are the means of conveying the communication.

Next, the path through which the message is to be transmitted can be termed as the channel. The channel may be through Letter, Phone, Telex, Fax or Internet. It depends upon the importance and urgency.

In the book 'My Presidential Years' Ex President of India Honbl Mr. R. Venkatraman has rightly mentioned that communication between him and the then Prime Minister Rajiv Gandhi was through a VIP suit case. One key was with him and the other with Rajiv only. Only through this closed locked suitcase all important matters were conveyed confidentially. This has been the channel for such high offices. So, channel in which the information flows is an important factor in communication. Decoding is nothing but realizing the meaning in it.

When a communication passes through several heads or agencies the decoding process suffers set back and it gets distorted.

Response and feedback are also back bones of communication.

If these are not in the proper texture then communication suffers.

The noise or disturbance usually interferes in the concept of correct communication.

Conveying through phones, telex etc have interference, which affects a good communication.

Communication also comprises verbal and non-verbal each having its own advantages and disadvantages.

Oral communications are Board Meetings, Officers Association Meetings, Telephone conversation etc.

Non-verbal is written communications such as memos, orders, etc, written in black and white.

Non-verbal communications will also be in the form of handshakes, smile, nodding etc, which conveys both good and bad.

Regarding channels we have the formal and informal communication.

A formal communication has the path intentionally prescribed and informal does not have this path.

A formal communication may be from boss to a subordinate in the downward direction or vice versa. This will be also lateral and diagonal.

They are in the orderly manner, when compared to informal communication.

Informal communication is not created by the organization and it spreads in all directions.

It has a tremendous speed and distortion.

It is like an assault of an employee by an officer, which will spread without any delay to various sections of the company like a forest fire.

A communication is a weapon, which has to be handled deftly by any manager and also by the organization.

Without proper utilization of the communication, there is bound to be a calamity in the organization with an irreparable loss.

What is Communication?

At the outset let us see what is meant by Communication?

Communication is the process by which all human interaction takes place.

The dictionary defines communication as the act of making oneself understood.

An expression of thoughts and opinions means of passing or sending information from one place to another.

Communication can be defined as the interchange of information ideas and opinions between and among people in any organization.

It is the process of passing information and understanding from one person to another.

Effective Communication involves both information and understanding.

We all started to communicate ever since we were born in this world.

Poor communication results in lowered morale, lowered production, excessive turnover, bad public relations and less efficient operation.

People differ in intelligence; education etc and so communication should be adapted to suit individual differences.

Manager wants one set of information, departmental head something else and employees at different ones.

Good communication is difficult to achieve, but all of us can benefit by improving our ability to communicate.

Communication is not an end in itself; it is the process by which ends are accomplished.

A company with good communication program creates good morale.

Purpose of Communication

One purpose of communication is to provide the information and understand necessary for group effort.

When people communicate they can work together.

The second purpose of communication is to provide the attitude necessary for motivation, co-operation and job satisfaction.

The purpose of communication is to impart among the people 'the skill to work' and also 'the will to work'.

Communication is used for:

-Orientation and induction of new employees

-Directing and commanding members of the organization

-Co-ordination

-Formal and informal interaction

Types of Communication:

Formal – Communication has delegated authority, responsibility and procedure

Informal – Arises from social interaction of the people.

Channels of Communication:

The channel of communication is the path over which communication travels. Three channels are

-Downward

-Upward

-Lateral

-Downward – from management to the operatives

-Upward – from subordinates to superiors

-Lateral – communication across divisions for coordination.

Having seen the elements of communication, now let us view the various barriers of communication.

Various types of barriers hamper the free flow of communication with an organization.

In upward communication, considerable amount of filtering takes place from one level to the other. It operates also in downwards and across communication.

Withholding of information and distortion do operate in the communication network.

Barriers:

-Inability to transmit and receive information properly

-Semantics in Communication

- Failure to understand the meaning is another barrier in communication.

-Fear, Suspicion and jealously

- Emotion also acts as a significant barrier in communication

-Immediate physical environment – example: Noise physical distance and presence of stranger may interfere with communication

-Psychological barrier with respect to age, sex and tradition also acts as barrier to communication. A manager has status and prestige different from that of workers. He talks and dresses differently. A worker cannot call a manager, whereas manager can call a worker.

Barriers to Effective Supervisory Communication:

Lack of Information:

The supervisor is the last to hear of news affecting the organization or the work group quite often. It is embarrassing for him to come to know certain developments from his employee or union representatives.

Bypassing of Supervisors:

Information frequently leaks from the top levels of the organization and goes directly to employees without informing the supervisor first. The union channel of communication is far more effective than communication to supervisors.

Supervisor Lacks Authority to Release Information:

Often the supervisors feel that they have responsibility without the authority to release information to the employees.

Management Practices:

-Overlaps in authority

-Poor methods of communication

-Failure to provide information to supervisors in all shifts

-Lack of sufficient personnel to communicate.

Working Conditions:

Work place are too busy and noisy for effective communication; both the supervisor and the employees are too busy to communicate; and so cannot go elsewhere to communicate effectively.

Attitude of Supervisors:

He himself may not be receptive to communication; he may be a poor listener; or he may not be willing to communicate when the information conflicts with his own point of view.

Attitude of Employees:

Employees' point of view, education, experience, language skill, habit, resistance, outside influence and frame of mind will have an effect on the supervisors' effects to communicate.

Steps to Overcome Communication Barriers

Installation of suggestion Boxes at vital points in the organization.

This will encourage one and all to express their views to improve communication barriers.

This act as a good morale booster!

Suggestion plans must have top management support.

Rewards should be given for good suggestions. This will encourage them to improve productivity efficiently.

Employee's suggestions should be prompt and certain and also rejections should be explained.

Advertisement in media for improvement and starting in-house magazines to publish the suggestions will do wonders.

Usage of Visual Methods:

Use of charts and graphs will help communication with facts and figures in a point blank manner.

A picture is worth thousand words or action. It speaks louder than words.

People believe in action or gestured communication more than picture or words.

Get Informed:

If a manager or supervisor does not know and understand, then he cannot communicate.

A manager or supervisor's span of information and understanding should be greater than his span of communication to his personnel.

Develop a Positive Communication Attitude:

The manager or supervisor should share information with employees to the extent they think and need it.

Plan for Communication:

Every plan of managerial action should have a plan for communicating it to those affected.

Gain the Acceptance of Others:

Meaning is more effectively communicated, when the receiver understands the purpose of communication.

Good Listening:

"A good listener is a good administrator"- G.R.D. Tata

Good listening helps the barrier to be shattered. Each and every instruction and vital points should be heard to take good decisions. Hearing with half heartedness will lead to improper communication.

-Have your mouth shut and ears open for success

- CEO. Kirloskar

'Learn by listening' said Deepak Parekh, Managing Director HDFC.

When a subordinate submits a report, he used to have a patient hearing even though he knew well ahead of his subordinates about all vital points.

"My boss listens not to know but to judge how many his subordinates knows"

-

says a CEO's secretary.

Building Trust:

When Rs 500 crores project was to be signed, the Chairman of Reliance Dhirubhai Ambani had only a 3 minute chat with his Managing Director and gave a signal saying "Take action what if I had been in your seat".

"Trust fetches trust" says Ambani.

Though the communication was short it had abundant juice of trust and hence communication gap was lessened and more effective.

Expression of Keenness and Enthusiasm:

By showing keenness the person who communicates will be enthused to speak more and hence good communication prevails.

"I am here to listen to your achievements and activities. My job is to listen and motivate you"--Swaraj Paul, Chairman Caparo Group.

So, showing eagerness and involvement in listening will make the subordinates sail smoothly.

Understanding the Feelings:

A man cannot understand full meaning of the words unless he understands the feelings of the person who uttered those. If a person discards the communicators' feelings then this will lead to a poor communication.

The entire motive behind the communication is lost. Morality will also be lost.

Asking Questions to You:

If you talk too much, ask yourself these questions:

-Do you explain your own position in excessive details?

-Do you plan answers while the other is still talking?

-Do you often get impatient while other is talking?

-Do you often miss the other's point?

If the answer is 'yes' to just one of those questions, then you are a mild case of verbosity.

Business Expressions:

A short list of expressions used in business to communicate effectively at the same time shortly.

-To expedite

-Under consideration

-To clarify

-To note and initial

-Let's get together on this

-Will advise you in due course

Calmness:

A popular press reporter had a chance of meeting Ex. Prime Minister Bharat Ratna Indira Gandhi for an exclusive interview for his journal.

As the interview was proceeding, the reporter asked very embarrassing and irritating questions about Sanjay Gandhi. Though it was too personal and out of the topic for which the interview was held, Smt. Indira Gandhi remained unperturbed and gave her views very politely and calmly without any sign of animosity.

"Her unique calmness astounded me" said the reporter in his biography "Her talents in communication was exemplary and unparalleled that she excelled as an outstanding figure in Indian Politics!"

Yes it's true!

Absolutely true!

Communication skills of Smt Indira Gandhi were a beacon light to one and all and every Indian woman should be proud and praise her at all times.

Four Step Method in Effective Communication:

Step I
-Planning

-Examine the true purpose of message.

-Seek to clarify your ideas for clarity and completeness.

-Use practical vocabulary as can be understood by the receiver (avoid technical and administrative jargon)

-Use more faces with reasons to replace guesses and inferences.

-Have a sense of balance in preparation of contents.

-Check the relevance of message for long range interests and goals of the organization and individual.

Tips

-Recognize what people mean.

-Recognize that there are no average learners.

-Consider the social and individual set up.

-Consult others for additional insight and objectivity.

-Be sincere and genuine.

-Observe principle of clarity.

Step 2

-Programming

-Inform right person at right time and place

-Speak clearly, slowly and deliberately.

-Control your tone of voice, facial expression and general mood.

-Write correctly and concisely

Tips
-Appreciate limitation of self and others.

-Create mutual confidence and friendly attitude.

-Be patient and enthusiastic

Step 3
-Feed Back

-Listen with interest and understanding of his reactions to what and why it is said.

-Watch for behavioral clues and detect overtones

-Insure understanding by encouraging questions.

-Don't anticipate, assume anything or get prejudiced.

-Don't be over anxious to show weaknesses or draw out conclusions

-Don't interrupt or do all the talking yourself.

-Be interested and open minded

-Observe principles of integrity.

Step 4

-Action

-Give adequate authority and support for actions

-Give encouragement for expression of reactions

-Convey something of help or value to strengthen efforts

-Check results by follow up contacts

-Review performance.

Tips

-Reinforce words with action

-Appreciate and admire results

-Be enthusiastic and helpful.

-Receiving or listening is important for good communication.

-Listening takes a considerable time in an Executive's job.

-A typical executive spends anywhere 35% to 55% of his time for receiving communication.

-Receiving process is a rewarding experience, as it opens the way for other man to talk freely.

-It implies understanding of what is said and also what is not said.

-It is an art of interpreting correctly the verbal response of the other man and to encourage him to express truly.

Barriers:

-Attributing bias and prejudices information may make the listener prejudiced about the person who speaks or the points he wishes to tell. Strained relations will set in motion the defensive mechanism for justification.

-Closing mind for other's views.

-If someone doesn't want his beliefs to get upset he can therefore turn the speaker off when he doesn't like what the other man says.

-Typical gestures and mannerisms may generate dislike.

Being Inattentive:

-Just as cricket enthusiast will most likely remember the various old cricket players' records than his school lessons, in the listening process too, one may hear only what one wants to hear or receive.

Drawing Unjustified Inferences:

-Tone and wording taken at face value without regard to the context may lead to incorrect inferences

-Forming judgment or evaluation of the speaker is important.

-One often guesses what the speaker is going to say before he speaks. Judging beforehand distracts mind from listening to what is really said.

-Appearance of facial expressions may arouse jealousy and anger.

-Plan

-Receive patiently – This requires putting oneself in other's shoes for understanding other person's emotions and suppressing one's ego. It means keeping mind open to views and ideas of others even though they are wrong or irrelevant.

-The processes involved in receiving and giving feedback are to be followed meticulously by all executives for smooth and congenial atmosphere. Any deviation will spark out unhealthy air and misunderstanding.

-The process of receiving and giving feedback could be vividly seen in Bhagawat Gita between Lord Krishna and Arjuna.

The inspiring dialogue delivered by Lord Krishna was well received with sincerity and devotion by Arjuna and the feedback was fantastic.

 It made him a jubilant warrior.

If there had been any set back between receiving and feedback, then the essence of vigor and strength would not have induced in the minds of Arjuna.

Exhilarating effects were seen as both the process worked well and that led to triumph of Arjuna.

So, also if a good coordination takes place in an organization in the receiving and feedback processes definitely success will come out in flying colors.

"In bringing about a change in large firms, it is not only their personal will to act that matters but a will to communicate and feedback effectively is vital"-**G.M.**

(HRD), Philips.